What It Means to Be a Christian

JOSEPH CARDINAL RATZINGER
(Pope Benedict XVI)

What It Means to Be a Christian

THREE SERMONS

Translated by Henry Taylor

IGNATIUS PRESS   SAN FRANCISCO

Title of the German original:
Vom Sinn des Christseins: Drei Predigten
© 1965 by Kösel-Verlag, Munich
New edition: 2005

Cover art: *Washing of the Feet* (detail of fresco)
Giotto di Bondone (1266–1336)
Scrovegni Chapel, Padua, Italy
© Scala / Art Resource, New York

Cover design by Roxanne Mei Lum

© 2006 Libreria Editrice Vaticana
© 2006 by Ignatius Press, San Francisco
All rights reserved
ISBN 978-1-58617-133-9
ISBN 1-58617-133-x
Library of Congress Control Number 2005933379
Printed in the United States of America ∞

Dedicated
with gratitude
and admiration
to
Romano Guardini

About This Book

The spoken word and the written word are so fundamentally different that there is always something questionable about making a spoken message into a book. If the author and the publisher have nonetheless decided to offer these sermons, which were preached to a congregation of Catholic students, to a wider public, then it is for the following reasons: first, the theme, in which the Advent dimension appears as a characteristic signature of Christian life and thought in general, is quite literally so necessary for our age that we believe we must snatch it from the transitoriness of the moment and offer it as the answer to many agonizing questions. Moreover, its original form, as the preached message of Christianity, adds a special and irreplaceable impetus to the bare contents. Our age, with its scientific abstractions, which sometimes seem to forget about living people, simply cannot afford to let this be lost.

Contents

Preface   11

First Sermon

Are We Saved? Or, Job Talks with God

Christianity as Advent   15
The Unfulfilled Promise   21
Are We Saved?   32
The Hidden God   35

Second Sermon

Faith as Service

The Salvation of Christians and the Salvation
    of the World   43
God Becomes Man, Man Becomes Christlike   50
The Meaning of Salvation History   56

Third Sermon

Above All: Love

Love Is Enough   65
Why Do We Need Faith?   72
The Law of Superabundance   77
Faith, Hope, and Love   84

Preface

This little book presents in written form three sermons that the author preached in the Cathedral at Münster to a congregation from the Catholic Student Chaplaincy, December 13–15, 1964. The response to my efforts once again to raise the question of what being Christian means for us in today's world and to answer that question, in the spoken words of these sermons, has encouraged me to publish them. I have consciously avoided going beyond the linguistic and material limitations inherent in the whole of this on account of its origin; with just a few alterations, it bears the form it took at the given moment. It is my hope that what I have said, in a form that makes no literary claims, may help in its own way toward that renewal of faith and proclamation which we so much need in a world that has fundamentally changed.

Joseph Ratzinger
Münster, Easter 1965

FIRST SERMON

Are We Saved?

or,

Job Talks with God

Christianity as Advent

In these weeks the Church is celebrating Advent, and we do so with her. If we try to think back to what we learned in our childhood about Advent and its meaning, we shall recall that we were told how the Advent wreath, with its candles, reminds us of the millennia (or perhaps, the thousands of centuries) of human history before Jesus Christ. That it reminds us, and the Church, of the time during which mankind, as yet unredeemed, was waiting for redemption. That it reminds us of the darkness of history that was still not yet redeemed, in which the lamps of hope were only gradually being lit, until finally Christ, the Light of the World, came and freed the world from its unredeemed darkness. Furthermore, we will think of how we learned that these millennia before Christ were the age of iniquity, on account of the Fall, whereas we learned to call the centuries after the birth of Christ *anni salutis reparatae*, the years of salvation restored. Finally, we will think of how we were told that in Advent, the Church is not only reflecting on the past, when it was Advent, the time of being unredeemed, of waiting, for all humanity; in Advent, the Church is, at the same time, looking beyond herself to the great multitude of those who have not yet been baptized, those for whom it is still "Advent", because they are still waiting and still living in unredeemed darkness.

If we, as people of our own century, with the experiences of this century, think further about such statements, as we once learned them, then we shall find it difficult to accept them completely. Will not the phrase about "the years of salvation"—supposedly the years since Christ's birth, as opposed to those before his birth—die upon our lips, seem indeed maliciously ironic, when we think about dates like 1914, 1918, 1933, 1939, 1945—dates that denote the period of world wars in which millions of people lost their lives, often in the most horrific circumstances; dates that recall memories of appalling deeds that humanity could not have committed earlier for purely technical reasons? Moreover, they include the date that reminds us of the beginning of a regime that elevated mass murder to a horrifying degree of perfection; and finally comes the memory of the year in which the first atomic bomb was detonated over a city full of people and in which the lurid light of an entirely new opening for darkness was manifested to the world.

When we reflect on such things, we shall simply no longer be able to divide history into ages of salvation and of iniquity. If we then extend our vision and look at what Christians (that is, those people we call "redeemed") achieved in the world by way of iniquity and devastation, in our own century and the previous centuries, then we will be equally incapable of dividing the peoples of the world into those who are saved and those who are not. If we are honest, we will no longer be able to paint things black and white, dividing up both history and maps into zones of salvation and iniquity. History as a whole, and mankind as a whole, will appear to us rather as a mass of gray, in which

time and again there appear flickers of that
goodness which can never quite be extin-
guished, in which, time and again, men set out
toward something better, but in which also, time
and again, collapses occur into all the horrors of
evil.

Yet when we reflect like this, it becomes plain
that Advent is not (as might perhaps have been
said in earlier ages) a sacred game of the liturgy,
in which, so to speak, it leads us once more
along the paths of the past, gives us once more a
vivid picture of the way things once were, so
that we may all the more joyfully and happily
enjoy today's salvation. We should have to admit,
rather, that Advent is not just a matter of re-
membrance and playing at what is past—Advent
is our present, our reality: the Church is not just
playing at something here; rather, she is refer-
ring us to something that *also* represents the
reality of our Christian life. It is through the
meaning of the season of Advent in the Church's
year that she revives our awareness of this. She
should make us face these facts, make us admit
the extent of being unredeemed, which is not
something that lay over the world at one time,

and perhaps somewhere still does, but is a fact in our own lives and in the midst of the Church.

It seems to me that we quite often run a particular risk: that of not wanting to see these things. We live with shades down over our windows, so to speak, because we are afraid that our faith could not stand the full, glaring light of the facts. So we shield ourselves against this and push these facts out of our consciousness, so as to avoid falling on our face. But a faith that will not account for half of the facts or even more is actually, in essence, a kind of refusal of faith, or, at least, a very profound form of scepticism that fears faith will not be big enough to cope with reality. It dares not accept the fact that faith is the power that overcomes the world. In contrast to that, true believing means looking the whole of reality in the face, unafraid and with an open heart, even if it goes against the picture of faith that, for whatever reason, we make for ourselves. That is why daring to talk to God out of the trial of our darkness, as Job did, is a part of Christian life. It is not part of that life for us to suppose we can present only half of our existence to God and have to spare him the rest because we might perhaps annoy him. No, it is precisely to him that we can and we must bring, in complete honesty, the whole burden of our life. We are rather too inclined to forget that in the Book of Job, handed down to us in Holy Scripture, at the end of the drama God declares Job to be righteous—Job, who has hurled the most outrageous accusations at God—while he rejects Job's friends as speakers of falsehood, those friends who had defended God and had found some kind of good sense and answer for everything.

Observing Advent simply means talking with God the way Job did. It means just seeing the whole reality and burden of our Christian life without fear and bringing it before the face of God, as judge and savior, even if, like Job, we have no answer to give about it all, and the only thing left is to leave it to God himself to answer and to tell him how we are standing here in our darkness with no answers.

The Unfulfilled Promise

Let us just try, then, in this time of Advent, to reflect before the face of God on the whole reality of Advent, which is not a game, but the factual dimension of our Christian life. In each person's case, based on *his* experience of life, those reflections will be different. I will merely take up a couple of images and ideas from Holy Scripture that may give a clear indication of the form in which questions oppress us today, in what way we experience the reality of Advent, though not in order to conduct a common analysis, but as one attempt at our struggling talk with God.

We find for instance in the Book of the prophet Isaiah (in chapter 11) the vision of the messianic age when the shoot of David, the Redeemer, will come. It says of that time,

The wolf shall dwell with the lamb,
   and the leopard shall lie down with the kid,

and the calf and the lion and the fatling
    together,
  and a little child shall lead them.
The cow and the bear shall feed;
  their young shall lie down together;
and the lion shall eat straw like the ox.

The sucking child shall play over the hole of
    the asp,
  and the weaned child shall put his hand on
    the adder's den.
They shall not hurt or destroy
  in all my holy mountain;
for the earth shall be full of the knowledge of
    the Lord
  as the waters cover the sea (Is 11:6–9).

We see how the time of the Messiah is depicted as a return of Paradise. We can, of course, say that a great deal here is just an image. For having bears and lambs, and lions and cows, tolerate one another is of course a metaphorical vision that is meant to express something more profound. We shall not in the least expect that anything like that must happen in our world. But this passage takes us far beyond that: in this image, it

is talking about the peace that will be characteristic of redeemed mankind. It is talking about
how redeemed people will be people of peace;
how they no longer act in an evil or malicious
way, because the land is filled with the knowledge of God, which covers the earth as water
does. Redeemed people—as this passage shows
us—live on the basis of their closeness to God
and on his reality, so that quite of their own
accord they become people of peace.

Yet what has become of this vision in the
Church, among us who call ourselves "redeemed"? We all know that it has not been
fulfilled, that the world has remained—has more
than ever become—a place of strife where there
is no peace, a world that lives from the conflict
of men with each other, a world branded by the
law of malice, of enmity, and of selfishness; a
world, furthermore, in which the knowledge of
God does not cover the land like water but
which lives in a state of being far from God, of
having God blacked out.

That may lead us to a second thought, which
arises when we read the prophecy of the New
Covenant in the Book of Jeremiah. It says there,

"This is the covenant which I will make with the house of Israel after those days, says the LORD: I will put my law within them, and I will write it upon their hearts" (Jer 31:33). And the same thing is found even more clearly in Isaiah: "All your sons shall be taught by the LORD" (Is 54:13). That is taken up in the New Testament, in chapter 6 of the Gospel of John, by the Lord himself, who describes the New Covenant as the time in which people no longer need to talk to each other about God, because each one is filled from within by the reality of God (Jn 6:45). It is taken up again in the Acts of the Apostles, in Saint Peter's address on the Day of Pentecost, when he recalls a similar prophecy by the prophet Joel and says that Joel's oracle—that in the last times God would pour out his spirit upon all flesh, "And your sons and your daughters shall prophesy" (Acts 2:16–21; Joel 2:28–32)—is now being fulfilled.

Once more, we have to say: How far we are from a world in which people no longer need to be taught about God because he is present within us! It has been asserted that our century is characterized by an entirely new phenomenon:

24

the appearance of people incapable of relating to God. As a result of spiritual and social develop-ments, it is said, we have reached the stage where a kind of person has developed in whom there is no longer any starting point for the knowledge of God. Whether that be true or not, we would have to admit that our distance from God—the obscurity and the dubiousness surrounding him today—is greater than ever before; indeed, that even we who are trying to be believers often feel as if the reality of God is being withdrawn from between our hands. Do we not ourselves often begin to ask where he is amid all the silence of this world? Do we not ourselves often have the feeling that, at the end of all our thinking, we have only *words* in our grasp, while the reality of God is farther away than ever before?

And that takes us to a further step. I believe the real temptation for someone who is a Chris-tian, as we experience it today, does not just consist in the theoretical question of whether God exists; or even the question of whether he is three or one; or even the question of whether Christ is God and man in one person. What really torments us today, what bothers us much more is the inefficacy of Christianity: after two thousand years of Christian history, we can see nothing that might be a new reality in the world; rather, we find it sunk in the same old horrors, the same despair, and the same hopes as ever. And in our own lives, too, we inevitably experience time and again how Christian reality is powerless against all the other forces that influence us and make demands on us. And if, after all our labor and efforts to live on the basis of what is Christian, we draw up the final balance sheet, then often enough the feeling comes over us that the reality has been taken away from us, dissolved, and all that remains in the end is just an appeal to the feeble light of our goodwill. And then in moments of discouragement like that, when we look back on the path we have traveled, the question forces its way into our minds: What is all this array of dogma and worship and Church, if at the end of it all we are still thrown back onto our own poor resources? That in turn brings us back again, in the end, to the question about the gospel of the Lord: What did he actually proclaim and bring among men? We will recall that, according to Saint Mark's account, Christ's message can be summed up in one saying: "The time is fulfilled, and the kingdom of God is at hand; repent, and believe in the gospel" (Mk 1:15).

"The time is accomplished: the kingdom of God has arrived." Behind this saying lies the whole history of Israel, that little people who had been a plaything for the great powers, who had sampled, so to speak, all the empires, one after another, that had ever arisen in that highly congested area of world history, and knew about the profligacy of any and every human rule, even that by their own people. They knew all too well that, wherever men rule, it is done in a very human way—that is, frequently in a very miserable and questionable fashion. Through this experience of a history full of disappointments, full of servitude and of injustice, there had grown up in Israel the demand for a kingdom that would not be any human rule, but the kingdom of God himself; the kingdom of God, in which he, the true ruler of the world and of history, would reign supreme. *He*, who is himself truth and righteousness, ought to rule everyone, so that well-being and justice among men should at last really be the only ruling powers. The Lord is responding to the hopes accumulated over centuries when he says: The time is now here; the kingdom of God has come. It is not difficult to understand the hopes aroused by such a saying. And our own disappointment, which sweeps over us when we look back at what has happened, is just as understandable.

Christian theology, which was very soon confronted by this discrepancy between expectation and fulfillment, in the course of time turned the kingdom of God into a kingdom of heaven that is beyond this mortal life; the well-being of men became a salvation of souls, which again comes to pass beyond this life, after death. But theology did not thereby provide an answer. For what is sublime in this message is precisely that the Lord was talking not just about another life, not just about men's souls, but was addressing the body, the whole man, in his embodied form, with his involvement in history and society; that he promised the kingdom of God to the man who lives bodily with other men in this history. As marvelous as the knowledge is that has been opened up for us by biblical scholarship in our century (that is, that Christ was not just looking forward to another life, but was talking about real people), it can also disappoint and unsettle us when we look at real history, which is in truth no kingdom of God.

We could pursue this thought by looking at the moral message of Jesus, at the words of the Sermon on the Mount, in which a straightforward call to be good is set against the casuistry of the Pharisees, and it is said, for instance, "You have heard that it was said to the men of old, 'You shall not kill; and whoever kills shall be liable to judgment.' But I say to you that every one who is angry with his brother shall be liable to judgment; whoever insults his brother shall be liable to the council, and whoever says, 'You fool!' shall be liable to the hell of fire" (Mt 5:21–22). When we hear words like these from the Sermon on the Mount, we are no doubt struck by the simplicity with which the moral tricks of casuistry are pushed aside. The simplicity with which a moral theology is set aside that was trying, so to say, to make it possible for men to get the better of God with clever tricks and to achieve salvation for themselves. We are struck by the simplicity with which straightforward assent to good itself is demanded, not assent to some law. But then, when we look more closely at sayings such as "Whoever says, 'You fool,' to his brother, shall be liable to the fire", they still strike us at the same time as a dreadful judgment, and the Pharisees' casuistry seems to us almost, by contrast, a kind of mercy, which is at least trying to accommodate the law to human weakness.

We might think, in such a reflection, of how Christ talked about the Old Testament dignitaries and about his own disciples; how he asked that no one be given any title any more, so that all should be like brothers and sisters because they have life from one Father (Mt 23:1–12). How often, in our thoughts, have we compared such words to the reality as we find it in the Church, all the various ranks and gradations that have been thought up, all the courtly ceremony! Yet there are things that go deeper than questions of outward form, which we should not dismiss yet also not overrate. Has not the New Testament ministry, we have to ask, fallen short of its true self, even in its essential nature? Did not Augustine have to say to his faithful that even for bishops in the Church, quite often the severe saying is true that the Lord uttered concerning the servants of the Old Covenant, "The scribes and the Pharisees sit on Moses' seat; so practice and observe whatever they tell you, but not what they do; for they preach, but do not practice. They bind heavy burdens, hard to bear, and lay them on men's shoulders; but they themselves will not move them with their finger" (Mt 23:2–4).

Are We Saved?

Let us take a further step, from Scripture to theology, and ask how that has explained "redemption"! We come upon the two paths it has taken, that of Western theology and that of Eastern. The theology of the West thought out a precise system: it says that God has been infinitely offended by sin, so that an infinite satisfaction was necessary. This infinite satisfaction, which no finite man could make, was achieved, it says, by Christ, the God-man. The individual receives this redemption through faith and baptism, so that he is pardoned with respect to original sin, which is prior to all particular sins and which is irredeemable by himself alone. He has to stand on his own, however, on the new ground that has thereby been won. When he steps into the arena of Christian life, he cannot get rid of the feeling that in this system grace seems to be referred to a sphere that has nothing to do with him personally, and he himself, in his moral struggles, seems to be left bereft of grace, at the mercy of his own achievements and merits. Thus, in the system, the idea of redemption is in fact salvaged, yet it has no effect in life; rather, it stands somewhere in the background, in the realm of a magnitude of infinite offense and satisfaction that is impossible for us to grasp, while our own existence stands amid the same difficulties and temptations as if this whole construct were simply not there.

Eastern theology explained redemption as the victory won by Christ over sin, death, and the devil. These world powers were defeated by the Lord once and for all, it says, and thus he redeemed the world. But again, when we look at the reality of our lives, who would still dare to maintain that the power of sin has been defeated? We know only too well, from our own lives and the temptations we meet, how much power it still wields. And who could seriously pronounce that death has been overcome? Here perhaps we meet the most common human aspect of man's lack of redemption: we are still subject to the power of death and to its constant presence in all our illness, weakness, loneliness, and affliction.

The Hidden God

It is Advent. And when we think upon everything we have to say, talking with God as Job did, then we really do feel in all its urgency how very genuinely it is still Advent, even for us. I think that we should first of all simply accept this. Advent is a reality, even for the Church. God has not divided history into a light half and a dark one. He has not divided people into those who are redeemed and those he has forgotten. There is only one, indivisible history, and it is characterized as a whole by the weakness and wretchedness of man, and as a whole it stands beneath the merciful love of God, who constantly surrounds and supports this history.[1]

---

[1] I have tried to show in my professorial dissertation, *Die Geschichtstheologie des heiligen Bonaventura* (Munich and Zürich, 1959) [reprinted with preface, St. Ottilien, 1992; English trans.: *The Theology of History in St. Bonaventure* (Chicago: Franciscan Herald Press, 1971), reprinted, 1989], that this was what was

Our century is making us learn anew the truth of Advent: that is, the truth that it has always been Advent and yet also still is Advent. That all mankind is one before God's face. That all mankind stands in darkness, but, on the other hand, that all mankind is illuminated by God's light. Yet if this is the way it is, that it has always been Advent and still is Advent, then this also means that there is no period of history for which God would be just the past, which already lies behind us and in which everything has already been done. On the contrary, for all of us God is the origin from which we come and yet

believed concerning the theology of history throughout the first millennium of Christianity. The division of history into "before Christ" and "after Christ", into redeemed and unredeemed time, that seems to us nowadays the essential expression of the Christian consciousness of history, for we think we cannot formulate any concept of the redemption, thus of the keystone of Christianity, without it—this division of history into periods is in fact simply the result of the great change in thinking about the theology of history that occurred in the thirteenth century. This was prompted by the writings of Joachim of Fiore; his teaching about the three epochs was indeed rejected, but the understanding of the Christ-event as a point in time separating different periods within history was adopted from him. The change in the overall understanding of everything to do with Christianity that results from this has to be seen as one of the most significant turnarounds in the history of Christian consciousness. A reappraisal of this will constitute an urgent task for theological study in our time.

still also the future toward which we are going. And that means, furthermore, that for all of us God cannot be found except by going to meet him as the One who is coming, who is waiting for us to make a start and demanding that we do so. We cannot find God except in this exodus, in going out from the coziness of our present situation into what is hidden: the brightness of God that is coming. The image of Moses, who had to climb up the mountain and go into the cloud to find God, remains valid for all ages. God cannot be found—even in the Church— except by our climbing the mountain and entering into the cloud of the incognito of God, who in this world is the hidden One. At the beginning of the New Testament salvation history, the same thing was intimated, in another way, to the shepherds at Bethlehem. They were told, "This will be a sign for you: you will find a baby wrapped in swaddling cloths and lying in a manger" (Lk 2:12). In other words, the sign for the shepherds is that they will meet, *not* with any sign, but simply the God who has become a child—and they will have to believe in the presence of God in this hiddenness. Their "sign"

37

demands that they learn to discover God in the incognito in which he is hidden. Their "sign" demands that they recognize that God is not to be found in the comprehensible systems of this world but can only be found at times when we grow beyond them.

Certainly, God has given a sign of himself in the greatness and power of the cosmos, from which we may dimly perceive something of the power of the Creator. But the real sign that he chose is hiddenness, from the wretched people of Israel to the child at Bethlehem to the man who died on the Cross with the words, "My God, my God, why have you forsaken me?" (Mt 27:46). This sign of hiddenness points us toward the fact that the reality of truth and love, the actual reality of God, is not to be met within the world of quantities but can be found only if we rise above that into a new order.[2] Pascal expressed this idea in his marvelous doctrine of the three orders. According to him, there is first of all the order of quantities—and that is enor-

[2] I owe the notion of the two signs of God—creation and being hidden in history—to an essay by P. Dessauer, "Geschöpfe von fremden Welten", *Wort und Wahrheit* 9 (1954): 569–83.

mous and infinite, the inexhaustible object of natural science. Beside that, the order of mind, the second great realm of reality, appears, on the basis of quantity, as simply nothing, since quantitatively it takes up no space whatever. And nonetheless, a single mind (Pascal mentions the mathematical mind of Archimedes as an example)—a single mind, as we were saying, is greater than the entire order of the quantitative cosmos; because mind, which has neither weight nor length nor breadth, is able to measure the entire cosmos. Yet above that, again, stands the order of love. That, too, is, in the first instance, simply nothing in the order of "mind", of scientific intelligence, as represented by Archimedes, since it cannot be the object of scientific demonstration and itself contributes nothing to any such demonstration. And nonetheless, a single motion of love is infinitely greater than the entire order of "mind", because only that represents what is a truly creative, life-giving, and saving power.[3] God's incognito is intended to

[3] Pascal, *Pensées*, no. 308 (ed. Lafuma) [ed. Brunschvicg, no. 793; English trans. in Everyman's Library, no. 874, pp. 234–35, no. 792]; cf. R. Guardini, *Christliches Bewußtsein* (Munich, 1950), pp. 40–46.

lead us onward into this "nothing" of truth and love, which is nevertheless in reality the true, single, and all-embracing absolute, and that is why in this world he is the hidden One and cannot be found anywhere else but in hiddenness.

It is Advent. All our answers remain fragmentary. The first thing we have to accept is, ever and again, this reality of an enduring Advent. If we do that, we shall begin to realize that the borderline between "before Christ" and "after Christ" does not run through historical time, in an outward sense, and cannot be drawn on any map; it runs through our own hearts. Insofar as we are living on a basis of selfishness, of egoism, then even today we are "before Christ". But in this time of Advent, let us ask the Lord to grant that we may live less and less "before Christ", and certainly not "after Christ", but truly *with* Christ and in Christ: with him who is indeed Christ yesterday, today, and forever (Heb 13:8).

Amen.

SECOND SERMON

Faith as Service

The Salvation of Christians
and the Salvation of the World

Saint Ignatius of Loyola, who outlined in his little book of Spiritual Exercises the path of his conversion from worldly service to the service of Jesus Christ, encourages the person who is willing to accompany him along this path in the Exercises to reflect, on first day of the second week, on the fundamental Christian mystery of the Incarnation of God. As is customary in this kind of meditation, he suggests that this person first visualize for himself the situation that constitutes the background to this event. It says about this, in the little book of Exercises, "The first thing to focus on is visualizing the event on which I am to meditate. In this case, it is how the three Divine Persons looked out over the whole surface or globe of the earth, full of people, and seeing how all of them were going down to hell, decided in their eternity that the second Person

43

should make himself a man, in order to save the human race; and when the fullness of time had come, they sent the angel Gabriel to our Lady." Ignatius sees before him a world that, without hope of salvation, has been given up to eternal damnation in hell.

The idea that all the people before Christ, and all those after him who remained outside the faith of the Church, suffer this fate was certainly one of the principal factors that motivated him to devote himself thenceforward with such fervor to the ministry of preaching the gospel. We can see how important this truly agitating— indeed, dreadful—thought was for him by the way that it comes again twice more in the same meditation. Twice more, the person who is reflecting is urged to look down upon the world through the eyes of God, so as to see how, up until the Incarnation of Christ, all men went down to hell.[1] The feeling of being profoundly disturbed, which must be aroused by such an idea, and the impulse of service to men that is released by it also underlie the work of the

[1] On all this, see Ignatius of Loyola, *Die Exerzitien*, trans. H. U. von Balthasar (Einsiedeln, 1959), pp. 33f.

great Jesuit missionary Francis Xavier. He carried out the Spiritual Exercises in the spirit of the head of his order, and much struck by such experiences as this, he went out to preach the word of God in all the world and to save as many men as possible from the terrible fate of eternal damnation.[2]

If we wanted to try to replicate Saint Ignatius' meditation today, then we would very quickly realize that we were simply unable any longer to think through the chain of thought we have just described. Everything we believe about God, and everything we know about man, prevents us from accepting that beyond the limits of the Church there is no more salvation, that up to the time of Christ all men were subject to the fate of eternal damnation. We are no longer ready and able to think that our neighbor, who is a decent and respectable man and in many ways better than we are, should be eternally damned simply because he is not a Catholic. We are no longer ready, no longer willing, to think that eternal

[2] J. Brodrick, *Abenteurer Gottes: Leben und Fahrten des heiligen Franz Xaver* (Stuttgart, 1954), esp. pp. 88f. (German trans. of *Saint Francis Xavier 1506–1552* [London: Burns, Oates, 1952]).

corruption should be inflicted on people in Asia, in Africa, or wherever it may be, merely on account of their not having "Catholic" marked in their passport. Actually, a great deal of thought had been devoted in theology, both before and after Ignatius, to the question of how people, without even knowing it, in some way belonged to the Church and to Christ and could thus be saved nevertheless. And still today, a great deal of perspicacity is used in such reflections.

Yet if we are honest, we will have to admit that this is not our problem at all. The question we have to face is not that of whether other people can be saved and how. We are convinced that God is able to do this with or without our theories, with or without our perspicacity, and that we do not need to help him do it with our cogitations. The question that really troubles us is not in the least concerned with whether and how God manages to save *others*.

The question that torments us is, much rather, that of why it is still actually necessary for *us* to carry out the whole ministry of the Christian faith—why, if there are so many other ways to heaven and to salvation, should it still be demanded of us that we bear, day by day, the whole burden of ecclesiastical dogma and ecclesiastical ethics? And with that, we are once more confronted, though from a different approach, with the same question we raised yesterday in conversation with God and with which we parted: What actually is the Christian reality, the real substance of Christianity that goes beyond mere moralism? What is that special thing in Christianity that not only justifies but compels us to be and live as Christians?

It became clear enough to us, yesterday, that there is no answer to this that will resolve every contradiction into incontrovertible, unambivalent truth with scientific clarity. Assent to the hiddenness of God is an essential part of the movement of the spirit that we call "faith". And one more preliminary consideration is requisite. If we are raising the question of the basis and meaning of our life as Christians, as it emerged for us just now, then this can easily conceal a sidelong glance at what we suppose to be the easier and more comfortable life of other people, who will "also" get to heaven. We are too much like the workers taken on in the first hour whom

47

the Lord talks about in his parable of the workers
in the vineyard (Mt 20:1–6). When they realized
that the day's wage of one denarius could be
much more easily earned, they could no longer
see why they had sweated all day. Yet how could
they really have been certain that it was so much
more comfortable to be out of work than to
work? And why was it that they were happy
with their wages only on the condition that
other people were worse off than they were? But
the parable is not there on account of those
workers at that time; it is there for our sake. For
in our raising questions about the "why" of
Christianity, we are doing just what those workers did. We are assuming that spiritual "unem-
ployment"—a life without faith or prayer—is
more pleasant than spiritual service. Yet how do
we know that?

We are staring at the trials of everyday Christianity and forgetting on that account that
faith is not just a burden that weighs us down;
it is at the same time a light that brings us
counsel, gives us a path to follow, and gives us
meaning. We are seeing in the Church only the
exterior order that limits our freedom and

thereby overlooking the fact that she is our spiritual home, which shields us, keeps us safe in life and in death. We are seeing only our own burden and forgetting that other people also have burdens, even if we know nothing of them. And above all, what a strange attitude that actually is, when we no longer find Christian service worthwhile if the denarius of salvation may be obtained even without it! It seems as if we want to be rewarded, not just with our own salvation, but most especially with other people's damnation—just like the workers hired in the first hour. That is very human, but the Lord's parable is particularly meant to make us quite aware of how profoundly un-Christian it is at the same time. Anyone who looks on the loss of salvation for others as the condition, as it were, on which he serves Christ will in the end only be able to turn away grumbling, because *that* kind of reward is contrary to the loving-kindness of God.

God Becomes Man,
Man Becomes Christlike

Thus, our question cannot be that of why God is able to save "others". That is his business, not ours. Yet we certainly can, and should, try to give some thought each day—within all the limitations that our reflections thus far have led us to recognize, of course— to what the point of *our* being Christians is, why God has called *us* to be believers. This, in turn, is just another form of the question of what the point of God's Incarnation actually was: Why did he come into the world if he did not change it, if, after him, it did not turn into a redeemed world?

We already touched on a first attempt at an answer yesterday. The power of Christ, we said, goes beyond anything that a division of the world into "redeemed" and "unredeemed" periods will admit; his power is more generous than that. It reaches out, not just to those who come *after* him (and how strange that would be!), but to everyone, and of course it puts everyone in the position of being free to make his own response. The Church Fathers were not in fact familiar with that expression, so commonly used by us, of the change of ages, of the "midpoint" of the ages, at which Christ is said to have come; they talked about Christ's having come at the *end* of the ages. What that means is that he is the goal and the basic underlying meaning of the *whole*.[1]

We may perhaps be able to visualize this in a new way, within our contemporary view of the world. Today, the world seems to us no longer a solid, well-ordered dwelling place, in which each thing has its proper place from the start and in which everything is forever firmly standing in its place, as it was made. To us, the world seems rather like a single great movement of things coming into being, like a symphony of being, which is developing step by step over time.

If we try, so far as is humanly possible, to follow in our minds the crescendos and diminuendos of this symphony of becoming, in its

[1] Bibliographical information is available in my book (see p. 35, n. 1).

wealth and in its failures, we shall be able to note one point in it that seems a decisive turning point for this cosmic symphony, a point at which something quite new begins, and yet something already intended and secretly at work as an underlying theme: I mean the point at which mind became aware for the first time in the world, when consciousness arose, not just being there, like other things, but being capable of thinking about itself and the world, capable of looking out toward eternity, toward God. Everything that had happened previously was given new meaning by the fact that mind now arose. It now appeared as a preparation for this breakthrough; mind took it into its service and thus gave it a new significance. And yet, if the human mind alone were in existence, then the movement of the cosmos would in the end be just a tragic course into vacuity, because we all know that man alone is unable to give himself, or the world, any sufficient meaning.

If, meanwhile, we look at the world in faith, we know that there is another, second break-through point within it: the moment at which God became man, the moment at which was achieved, not just the breakthrough from nature to mind, but the breakthrough from Creator to creature. That is the moment when, in one place, the world and God became one. The significance of all the history that followed after can only be that of including the entire world within this union and, on that basis, giving it the fulfilled meaning of being at one with its Creator. "God became man, in order that men might become gods", is what Saint Athanasius, Bishop of Alexandria, said. We can say, as a matter of fact, that the actual meaning of history is being announced to us here. In the breakthrough from the world to God, everything that went before and everything that followed afterward is given its proper significance as the great movement of the cosmos is drawn into the process of deification, into a return to the state from which it originated.

If at this point we take our thought a little farther and look at ourselves, it becomes apparent that what seems at first to be perhaps just some speculation or other about the world and things in general includes a quite personal program for us ourselves. For man's awesome alternative is either to align himself with this movement, thus obtaining for himself a share in the meaning of the whole, or to refuse to take this direction, thereby directing his life into meaninglessness. Now being a Christian simply means giving our assent to this movement and putting ourselves at its service. Becoming a Christian is not taking out an individual insurance policy; it is not the private booking of an entry ticket for heaven, so that we can look across at other people and say, "I've got something the others haven't got; I've got salvation arranged for me that they don't possess." Becoming a Christian is not at all something given to us so that we, each individual for himself, can pocket it and keep our distance from those others who are going off empty-handed. No: in a certain sense, one does not become a Christian for oneself at all; rather, one does so for the sake of the whole, for others, for everyone. The movement of becoming a Christian, which begins at baptism and which we have to pursue through the rest of our lives, means being ready to engage in a particular service that God requires from us in history. We cannot of course always think through in detail why this service has to be done by me, now, in this way. That would contradict the mystery of history, which is woven together from the inscrutability of man's freedom and God's freedom. It should be enough for us to know in faith that we, by becoming Christians, are making ourselves available for a service to the whole. Thus, becoming a Christian does not mean grabbing something for oneself alone; on the contrary, it means moving out of that selfishness which only knows about itself and only refers to itself and passing into the new form of existence of someone who lives for others.

The Meaning of Salvation History

It is on this plane that we have to understand everything to do with Christian "salvation history". Only in that way can we understand Holy Scripture at all. If we look at the Old Testament, at the election of Israel: God did not take Israel in order to concern himself just with that one people and to leave all the others to their own devices. He took hold of it in order to use it for a particular service. And so it is, in turn, if we look at Christ and the Church. Here again, it is not a matter of some people being loved by God and others being forgotten by him; rather, it is a matter of everyone being there for the sake of one another. The mystery of Israel and the mystery of the Church are both intended to teach us one and the same thing: that God wants to come to men only through other men. That he does not send his lightning down vertically upon the individual, so that faith and religion would be worked out simply between him and that individual. He intends, rather, to construct the meaning of history in our service to one another and with one another. Thus, being a Christian means, constantly and in the first instance, letting ourselves be torn away from the selfishness of someone who is living only for himself and entering into the great basic orientation of existing for the sake of another.

All the great images in Holy Scripture signify this, fundamentally. The image of the Pascha, which is fulfilled in the New Testament mystery of the death and Resurrection; the image of the exodus, of going out from what is familiar, what is our own, which begins with Abraham and remains a fundamental rule of salvation history through all time: everything is intended to express this one basic movement of freeing oneself from existing merely for one's own sake. Christ the Lord expressed it most profoundly in the rule about the grain of wheat, which shows, at the same time, that this fundamental law sets its mark, not only on the whole of history, but, even before that, on the whole of God's creation: "Truly, truly, I say to you, unless a grain of wheat falls into the earth and dies, it remains alone; but if it dies, it bears much fruit" (Jn 12:24).

In his death and his Resurrection, Christ fulfilled the law of the grain of wheat. In the Eucharist, in the Bread of God, he has truly become the fruit, multiplied a hundredfold, from which we are still living. Yet in this mystery of the Holy Eucharist, in which he is still constantly the One who is truly and entirely there for us, he challenges us to enter day by day into this law ourselves, which, in the final analysis, is merely the expression of the essence of true loving. For fundamentally, love cannot mean anything but this: that we allow ourselves to be parted from that narrow view directed toward our own ego and that we begin to move out from our own self, in order to be there for others. Ultimately, the basic movement of Christianity is simply the basic movement of love, through which we share in the creative love of God himself.

So when we say that the meaning of Christian service, the meaning of our Christian faith, cannot be determined solely on the basis of the individual believer, but, rather, that this meaning derives from taking an essential, indispensable place in the whole and for the sake of the whole; when we say that we are Christians, not for our own sakes, but because God wishes us, and needs us, to take on this service in the broad sweep of history, then we should not, nevertheless, fall into the opposite error of talking as though the individual were only a small cog in the great cosmic machine. Although it is true that God wants, not just individuals, but all of us in our relations with and for one another, it nonetheless remains true that he knows and loves every single one of us, for ourselves. Jesus Christ, the Son of God and Son of man, in whom there took place the decisive breakthrough of universal history toward the union of the creature with God, was an individual, born of a human mother. He lived a unique life, had his own personal face, and died his own death. What is both offensive and sublime in the Christian message is still that the fate of all history, our fate, depends on one individual: Jesus of Nazareth.

Both things become apparent at the same time in this one figure: how we are here for one another and live in dependence on one another; and how, nevertheless, God unmistakably knows and loves each individual distinctively. I think that both of these things together should make a deep impression on us. On the one hand, we should assimilate this way of understanding Christianity as existing for one another. Yet we should live no less from this great certainty, this great joy: that God loves *me*, this particular person; that he loves each one who has a human face, however disturbed and however distorted that human face might be. And when we say, "God loves me", we should not simply feel the responsibility, the danger of being unworthy of that love; rather, we should accept the message about love and grace in all its sublimity and its integrity.

The fact that God is kind and forgiving is no less included in this. Perhaps, because of a mistaken anxiety to make an educational and moral point, we have simply too completely neutralized the great parables about forgiveness in our preaching in the Church and have surrounded them with safeguards: the parable of the creditor who remits a debt of millions; the parable of the shepherd who goes after the one sheep that is lost; and that of the housewife who rejoices more over the drachma she has lost and then found again than over everything she has never lost at all. The boldness of the facts of Jesus' life in no way falls short of the boldness of these parables, for we find among his closest disciples the tax collector Levi and the whore Magdalen. Yet in the boldness of this message, both the things we need are nevertheless given: for anyone who really believes, it is clear that he will not use the certainty of divine forgiveness as license for complete lack of restraint, just as a lover does not make use of the fact that the other person's love is inextinguishable, but feels called upon by that very fact to do his best, for his own part, to become worthy of such love. Yet such an intention, which is aroused within us by our faith in that love, is based, not on fear, but on the full and joyful certainty that God is truly—and not just in pious phrases—greater than our own heart (1 Jn 3:20).

Perhaps it would be worthwhile, in conclusion, to consider again how Saint Ignatius' meditation would look today, if we were to take it up again in our own historical situation. The decisive point remains this: men are unable, of themselves, to give any meaning to their individual and collective stories. If they were left to their own devices, human history would run out into nothing, into nihilism, into meaninglessness. No one has grasped this more profoundly than the poets of our time, who feel and live in that solitude of man left to himself, who describe the boredom and pointlessness that are the basic sense of such a man who becomes a hell for himself and for others.

What else will remain is the knowledge that the whole of this has gained meaning through Christ, that in the breakthrough from the Creator to the creature, this movement into nothingness has become a movement into the fullness of eternal significance. Yet beyond what Ignatius suggests, nowadays we will include the insight that God's mercy, made manifest in Christ, is sufficiently abundant for everyone. It is so abundant that it even demands our participation as instruments of his mercy and his loving-kindness. That is why we are Christians. May God help us to be true Christians. Amen.

THIRD SERMON

Above All: Love

Love Is Enough

A story current in late Judaism, in Jesus' time, tells how one day a pagan came to Rabbi Shammai, the famous head of a school, and told him that he would be willing to join the Jewish religion if the Rabbi could tell him about its beliefs in the time someone could stand on one leg. The Rabbi probably thought in his mind about the five books of Moses, with all the ideas in them, and everything that Jewish interpretation had added in the meantime and had declared to be equally obligatory, necessary, and essential for salvation. As he went over all this in his mind, he finally had to admit that it would be impossible for him to summarize in a couple of sentences the whole of everything that made up the religion of Israel. The strange petitioner was not a whit discouraged. He went—if we want to put it like that—to the competition: to the other famous head of a school, Rabbi Hillel, and laid the same request before him. In contrast to Rabbi Shammai, Hillel found the suggestion in no way impossible and answered him straight out, "Whatever is offensive to you yourself, do not do that to your neighbor. That is the whole law. Everything else is interpretation."[1]

If the same man were to go today to some learned Christian theologian or other and ask him to give him, in five minutes, a brief introduction to the essence of Christianity, then probably all the professors would say that that was impossible: They would in any case need six semesters alone for the basic subject of theology; and even at that, they would scarcely have reached the edges. And yet again, it might be possible to help the man. For the story about Rabbis Hillel and Shammai was replayed, just a few decades after it had first taken place, in another form. This time, a rabbi stood before Jesus of Nazareth and asked him, "What must I do to achieve salvation?" This is the question of what Christ himself sees as absolutely essential in

---

[1] H. Strack and P. Billerbeck, *Das Evangelium nach Matthäus, erläutert aus Talmud und Midrasch* (Munich, 1922), p. 357.

his message. The Lord's reply was this: "You shall love the Lord your God with all your heart, and with all your soul, and with all your mind. This is the great and first commandment. And a second is like it, You shall love your neighbor as yourself. On these two commandments depend all the law and the prophets" (Mt 22:35–40). That, then, is the whole of Jesus Christ's demand. Anyone who does this—who has love —is a Christian; he has everything (see also Rom 13:9–10).

We can see from that other passage in which Christ depicts the Last Judgment in parabolic form that this is not meant by Christ as just a comforting way of speaking that should not be pushed too far; rather, it is to be understood in full seriousness, without reservations. The Judgment represents the real and ultimate thing; it is the test in which it is made clear how things really stand. For here man's eternal destiny is irrevocably decided. In the parable of the Last Judgment, the Lord says that the Judge will be confronted with two kinds of men. To one group he will say, "Come, O blessed of my Father, inherit the kingdom prepared for you from the foundation of the world; for I was hungry and you gave me food, I was thirsty and you gave me drink, I was a stranger and you welcomed me, I was naked and you clothed me, I was sick and you visited me, I was in prison and you came to me." And those people will say, "When did we do all this? We have never met you." Christ will answer them, "Truly, I say to you, as you did it to one of the least of these my brethren, you did it to me." With the other group, the opposite will happen. The Judge will say to them, "Depart from me, you cursed, into the eternal fire prepared for the devil and his angels; for I was hungry and you gave me no food, I was thirsty and you gave me no drink, I was a stranger and you did not welcome me, naked and you did not clothe me, sick and in prison and you did not visit me." And these people, too, will ask, "When was all this? If we had seen you, we would have given you everything." And to them, in turn, will be said, "As you did it not to one of the least of these, you did it not to me" (Mt 25:31–46). In this parable, the Judge does not ask what kind of theory a person has held about God and the world. He is not asking about a confession of dogma, solely about love. That is enough, and it saves a man. Whoever loves is a Christian.

However great the temptation may be for theologians to quibble about this statement, to provide it with ifs and buts, notwithstanding: we may and should accept it in all its sublimity and simplicity, quite unconditionally—just as the Lord posited it. That does not mean, of course, that we should overlook the fact that these words represent a not inconsiderable proposition and make no small demand on someone. For love, as it is here portrayed as the content of being a Christian, demands that we try to live as God lives. He loves us, not because we are especially good, particularly virtuous, or of any great merit, not because we are useful or even necessary to him; he loves us not, because *we* are good, but because *he* is good. He loves us, although we have nothing to offer him; he loves us, even in the ragged raiment of the prodigal son, who is no longer wearing anything lovable. To love in the Christian sense means trying to follow in this path: not just loving someone we like, who pleases us, who suits us, and certainly not just someone who has something to offer us or from whom we are hoping to gain some advantage.

Practicing Christian love in the same way as Christ means that we are good to someone who needs our kindness, even if we do not like him. It means committing ourselves to the way of Jesus Christ and thus bringing about something like a Copernican revolution in our own lives. For in a certain sense, we are all still living before Copernicus, so to speak. Not only in that we think, to all appearances, that the sun rises and sets and goes around the earth, but in a far more profound sense. For we all carry within us that inborn illusion by virtue of which each of us takes his own self to be the center of things, around which the world and everyone else have to turn. We all necessarily find ourselves, time and again, construing and seeing other things and people solely in relation to our own selves, regarding them as satellites, as it were, revolving around the hub of our own self. Becoming a Christian, according to what we have just said, is something quite simple and yet completely revolutionary. It is just this: achieving the Copernican revolution and no longer seeing ourselves as the center of the universe, around which everyone else must turn, because instead of that we have begun to accept quite seriously that we are one of many among God's creatures, all of which turn around God as their center.

Why Do We Need Faith?

Being a Christian means having love. That is unbelievably difficult and, at the same time, incredibly simple. Yet however difficult it may be in many respects, discovering this is still a profoundly liberating experience. You will probably say, however: Well and good, that is what Jesus' message is about, and that is very fine and comforting. But what have you theologians and priests made of it, what has the Church made of it? If love is enough, why do we have your dogma? Why do we have faith, which is forever competing with science? Is it not really true, then, what liberal scholars have said, that Christianity has been corrupted by the fact that, instead of talking with Christ about God the Father and being like brothers to each other, people have constructed a doctrine of Christ; by the fact that people, instead of leading others to mutual service, have invented an intolerant dogma; by the fact that instead of urging people to love, they have demanded belief and made being a Christian depend on a confession of faith?

There is no doubt that there is something terribly serious in this question, and like all really weighty questions, it cannot be dealt with just like that, with a well-turned phrase. At the same time, however, we cannot miss the fact that it also involves a simplification. To see this clearly, we need only realistically apply our reflections so far to our own lives. Being a Christian means having love; it means achieving the Copernican revolution in our existence, by which we cease to make ourselves the center of the universe, with everyone else revolving around us.

If we look at ourselves honestly and seriously, then there is not just something liberating in this marvelously simple message. There is also something most disturbing. For who among us can say he has never passed by anyone who was hungry or thirsty or who needed us in any way? Who among us can say that he truly, in all

simplicity, carries out the service of being kind
to others? Who among us would not have to
admit that even in the acts of kindness he prac-
tices toward others, there is still an element of
selfishness, something of self-satisfaction and
looking back at ourselves? Who among us would
not have to admit that he is more or less living in
the pre-Copernican illusion and looking at other
people, seeing them as real, only in their relationship to our own selves? Thus, the sublime
and liberating message of love, as being the sole
and sufficient content of Christianity, can also
become something very demanding.

It is at this point that faith begins. For what
faith basically means is just that this shortfall
that we all have in our love is made up by the
surplus of Jesus Christ's love, acting on our be-
half. He simply tells us that God himself has
poured out among us a superabundance of his
love and has thus made good in advance all our
deficiency. Ultimately, faith means nothing other
than admitting that we have this kind of shortfall;
it means opening our hand and accepting a gift.
In its simplest and innermost form, faith is nothing but reaching that point in love at which we

recognize that we, too, need to be given something. Faith is thus that stage in love which really distinguishes it as love; it consists in overcoming the complacency and self-satisfaction of the person who says, "I have done everything, I don't need any further help." It is only in "faith" like this that selfishness, the real opposite of love, comes to an end. To that extent, faith is already present in and with true loving; it simply represents that impulse in love which leads to its finding its true self: the openness of someone who does not insist on his own capabilities, but is aware of receiving something as a gift and of standing in need of it.

This faith is of course susceptible to many and varied developments and interpretations. We need only to become aware that the gesture of opening our hand, of being able to receive in all simplicity, through which love first attains its inner purity, is grasping at nothing unless there is someone who can fill our hands with the grace of forgiveness. And thus once again everything would have to end in idle waste, in meaninglessness, if the answer to this, namely, Christ, did not exist. Thus, true loving necessarily passes into the gesture of faith, and in that gesture lies a demand for the mystery of Christ, a reaching out toward it—and that mystery, when it unfolds, is a necessary development of that basic gesture; to reject it would be to reject both faith and love.

And yet, conversely, however true this may be—and however much christological and ecclesiastical faith is for that reason absolutely necessary—at the same time, it remains true that everything we encounter in dogma is, ultimately, just interpretation: interpretation of the one truly sufficient and decisive fundamental reality of the love between God and men. And it remains true, consequently, that those people who are truly loving, who are as such also believers, may be called Christians.

The Law of Superabundance

Starting from this basic understanding of Christianity, Scripture and dogma can be read and understood in a new way. I will mention only a couple of examples, passages from Holy Scripture that at first seem quite inaccessible to us and then, all at once, in this light, open up for us. Let us recall, for instance, the saying in the Sermon on the Mount that we met the day before yesterday in all its awesomeness: "You have heard that it was said to the men of old, 'You shall not kill; and whoever kills shall be liable to the judgment.' But I say to you that every one who is angry with his brother shall be liable to judgment; whoever insults his brother shall be liable to the council, and whoever says 'You fool!' shall be liable to the hell of fire" (Mt 5:21–22). Whenever we read this passage, it weighs on us; it crushes us. Yet there is a verse just before that gives the passage its whole meaning when it says, "I tell you, unless your righteousness exceeds that of the scribes and Pharisees, you will never enter the kingdom of heaven" (Mt 5:20). The key word in this verse is "exceeds". The original Greek is still more strongly expressed, and only that really shows the basic intention here. In literal translation, it says, "Unless your righteousness has more superabundance than that of the scribes and Pharisees. . . ."

Here we meet with a theme that runs through the whole of Christ's message. The Christian is the person who does not calculate; rather, he does something extra. He is in fact the lover, who does not ask, "How much farther can I go and still remain within the realm of venial sin, stopping short of mortal sin?" Rather, the Christian is the one who simply seeks what is good, without any calculation. A merely righteous man, the one who is only concerned with doing what is correct, is a Pharisee; only he who is not *merely* righteous is beginning to be a Christian. Of course, that does not, by a long way, mean that a Christian is a person who does nothing wrong and has no failings. On the contrary, he is the person who knows that he does have failings and who is generous with God and with other people because he knows how much he depends on the generosity of God and of his fellowmen. The generosity of someone who knows he is in debt to everyone else, who is quite unable to attempt to maintain a correctness that would allow him to make strict demands in return: that is the true guiding light of the ethical code that Jesus is proclaiming (cf. Mt 18:13–35). This is the mystery, at once incredibly demanding and liberating, to be found behind the word "superabundance", without which there can be no Christian righteousness.

If we look closer, we realize at once that the basic relationship we have discovered through the idea of "superabundance" is characteristic of the whole story of God's dealings with man, indeed, that it is, moreover, as it were, the characteristic trait of divinity in creation itself. The miracle at Cana and the miracle of feeding the five thousand are signs of that superabundance of generosity which is essential to God's way of acting, that way of doing things which in the process of creation squanders millions of

seeds so as to save *one* living one. That way of
doing things which lavishly produces an entire
universe in order to prepare a place on earth for
that mysterious being, man. That way of doing
things by which, in a final, unheard-of lavishness, he gives himself away in order to save that
"thinking reed", man, and to bring him to his
goal. This ultimate and unheard-of event will
always defy the calculating minds of correct
thinkers. It can really be understood only on the
basis of the foolishness of a love that discards any
notion of calculation and is unafraid of any
lavishness. And yet, again, it is no more than the
logical conclusion of that lavishness which is, as
it were, on all sides the personal stamp of the
Creator and is now likewise set to become the
basic rule for our own existence before God
and men.

Let us go back to what we were saying. We
said that, on the basis of this perception (which,
in turn, is only an application of the principle of
"love"), not only do the pattern of creation and
that of salvation history become comprehensible, but also the meaning of the demands Jesus
makes on us, as we meet them in the Sermon on

the Mount. It is certainly most helpful to know from the start that they are not to be understood in a legalistic sense. Teachings like this: "If any one strikes you on the right cheek, turn to him the other also; and if anyone . . . take your coat, let him have your cloak as well" (Mt 5:39f.) are not articles of law that we have to carry out as particular commands in a literal sense. They are not articles, but vivid examples and images, which, taken together, are intended to give direction. And yet that is not enough to arrive at a real understanding of them. We have to dig deeper for that and to see that in the Sermon on the Mount, on one hand, a merely moralistic interpretation—which understands everything that is said as commandments, so that if we do not keep them we will go to hell—is inadequate: seen like that, it would not raise us up but crush us. Yet, on the other hand, an interpretation merely in terms of grace is likewise inadequate, an interpretation asserting that all that is being shown here is how worthless all our human actions and activity are; that this merely makes clear that we can achieve nothing and that all is grace. Such an interpretation says that this

passage is just making it clear that in the night of
human sinfulness all distinctions are trivial and
that no one has any rights he can insist on,
anyway, because everyone deserves damnation
and everyone is saved only by grace. Certainly,
this passage makes us conscious, with appalling
clarity, of our need for forgiveness; it shows how
little reason any man has for boasting and for
setting himself apart from sinners as a righteous
man. But the point of it is something different. It
is not just intended to set us all against a background of judgment and forgiveness, which
would then make all human activity a matter of
indifference. It has another aim as well, which is
to give directions for our life: it is intended to
point us toward that "extra", that "superabundance" and generosity, which does not mean
that we suddenly become faultless and "perfect"
people, but it does mean that we try to adopt the
attitude of the lover, who does not calculate but
simply—loves.

And finally, the quite concrete christological
backdrop of the Sermon on the Mount is part of
this. The call for something "more" does not
simply ring out from the unapproachable and

eternal majesty of God; rather, it sounds forth from the mouth of the Lord, in whom God has given away his own self into the wretchedness of human history. God himself lives and works according to the rule of superabundance, of that love which can give nothing less than itself. That is the simple answer to the question about the essence of Christianity, which confronts us again at the end and which, properly understood, includes everything.

Faith, Hope, and Love

There is still one thing for us to think about at the end. Through talking about love, we came upon faith. We saw that, properly understood, faith is present within love and that only faith can bring love to its proper end, because our own loving would remain just as inadequate as an open hand stretched out into emptiness. If we think a little further, we also come upon the mystery of hope. For our believing and our loving are still on their way, so long as we remain in this world, and again and again they are in danger of flickering out. It is truly Advent. No one can say of himself, "I *am* completely saved." In the era of this world, there is no redemption as a past action, already completed; nor does it exist as a complete and final present reality; redemption exists only in the mode of hope. The light of God does not shine in this world except in the lamps of hope that his loving-kindness has set up on our way. How often that distresses us: we would like more; we would like the whole thing, round, unassailably present. Yet basically we have to say: Could there be any more human way of redeeming us than that which declares us to be beings in the course of development, on our way, that tells us we may hope? Could there be a better light for us, as nomadic beings, than the one that sets us free to go forward without fear, because we know that the light of eternal love stands at the end of the road?

Tomorrow, Wednesday, an Advent Ember Day, we shall encounter this very mystery of hope in the liturgy of the Holy Mass. The Church sets it before us on this particular day in the shape of the Mother of the Lord, the Blessed Virgin Mary. For these weeks of Advent she stands before us as the woman who is carrying the Hope of the world just under her heart and, thus, going before us on our way as a symbol of hope. She stands there as the woman in whom what is humanly impossible has become possible, through God's saving mercy. And thus she becomes a symbol for us all. For if it is up to us, if it depends on the feeble flame of our goodwill and the paltry sum of our actions, we cannot achieve salvation. However much we are capable of, it is not enough for that. It remains impossible. Yet God, in his mercy, has made the impossible possible. We need only say, in all humility, "Behold, I am a servant of the Lord" (cf. Lk 2:37f.; Mk 10:27). Amen.